My Success Journal

For Young People

THIRD EDITION
Updated and Expanded

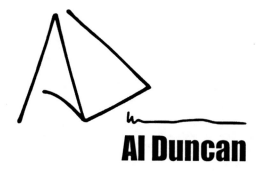

Al Duncan

Published by Al Duncan Publishing LLC

Library of Congress Cataloging-in-Publication Data

Duncan, Al
My success journal for young people/ by Al Duncan — 3rd edition
p. cm

ISBN13: 978-0-9831900-0-4
LCCN: 2011900157

1. Personal Development. 2. Self-Help. 3. Journal. 4. Teenagers.
5. Young Adults I. Title

To my sons, Mekhi and Ramses, my brother, Nate, and all the young people that I've ever trained or mentored. You all are my inspiration.

Contents

Wait! Before you start reading...
Have you seen your free bonuses?

FREE BONUSES FOR YOU

My Success Journal Video Series: A free video series to enhance your experience with exclusive insights and commentary by me, Al Duncan.
http://duncannuggets.com/success-journal-videos

Goal Achievement Collection: A free collection of videos, articles, posters, and activities focused on goal achievement. Designed for group or individual use.

Visit the *Collections and Series* page on
www.DuncanNuggets.com

Personal Branding Collection: A free collection of videos, articles, posters, and activities focused on personal branding. Designed for group or individual use.

Visit the *Collections and Series* page on
www.DuncanNuggets.com

Write and Succeed

"Keep a journal? You? Ain't diaries for girls?"

"Absolutely not. Name somebody famous that you have a lot of respect for."

"MJ."

"Michael Jordan? He kept a success journal. He called it his Dream Book."

"For real? But what am I supposed to write?"

"Come on. I'll show you."

—A conversation between Al Duncan and a female basketball player

I want to personally congratulate you for deciding to keep a success journal. You are now doing what countless other successful people have done—putting your dreams, goals, plans, and ideas on paper.

Some of the greatest individuals in the history of the world, such as Frederick Douglass and Leonardo DaVinci, kept journals. Although some called them diaries, like Anne Frank, or simply a list of goals and dreams, like Michael Jordan, they have one thing in common: they were more successful and happy because of writing things down.

In many cases, what they wrote also made the world a better place. Rachel Scott, the first student killed at the Columbine High School massacre in 1999, kept six diaries which have inspired millions of people through a program called Rachel's Challenge.

Carmelo Anthony, the All-Star basketball player, said that he used to sleep with his goals underneath his pillow. Oprah Winfrey has been journaling since she was 15 and Miley Cyrus says that she has a shelf full of personal journals.

Here are some well-known people that believed in the power of keeping journals and having goals. I call them *Trendsetters and Goal-Getters*:

TRENDSETTERS & GOAL-GETTERS

Muhammad Ali
3-time World Heavyweight
Boxing Champ, "The Greatest"

Oprah Winfrey
Media Mogul, Philanthropist

Charles Darwin
English Naturalist

Tyra Banks
Super Model, Businessperson

Jay Z
Hip-Hop Artist, Entrepreneur

Anthony Robbins
Professional Speaker, Author,
Entrepreneur

Mary Kay Ash
Founder of Mary Kay Cosmetics

Benjamin Franklin
One of the Founding Fathers of
the United Sates of America

Ernest Hemingway
American writer, journalist

George Orwell
Author of Animal Farm and
Nineteen Eighty Four

King Solomon
The Book of Proverbs,
Ecclesiastes, Song of Songs

Frederick Douglas
Abolitionist, Orator, Author

Aristotle
Greek Philosopher

Russell Simmons
Entrepreneur, Philanthropist

Ellen Ochoa
First Hispanic Woman
Astronaut

Helen Keller
Author, Activist, Lecturer

Samuel Pepys
English Naval Administrator
Member of Parliament

Will Smith
Film Producer, Actor, Rapper

Farrah Gray
Self-Made Millionaire by age
14, Author

Tiger Woods
Professional Golfer

Donald Trump
Billionaire Business Magnate,
TV Personality, Author

Sun Tzu
Author of The Art of War

...and the list goes on. Many of the U.S. presidents also kept diaries. Look for some other successful people who write down their goals and keep journals. There are plenty.

THE POWER OF PEN & PAPER

Duncan Nugget® #1:
Write and succeed.
Writing down what you want and how you plan to get it is crucial to your success. You are far more likely to do what it takes to achieve your dreams, goals, and aspirations if you plan it out in writing.

Writing helps you to think clearly and to better visualize achieving the goals you've set. Simply writing things down, however, won't guarantee success. Being successful requires the right combination of action, knowledge, determination, help, and self-discipline. Writing things down helps to create that combination.

The bottom line is:

You tend to accomplish a lot more by putting your dreams, goals, plans, and ideas on paper.

Let's take a look at a famous study of Yale graduates. In 1953, researchers interviewed the graduating seniors at Yale University and asked them if they had a set of written goals. Less than 3% of the graduates had their goals written down on paper.

In 1973, twenty years later, a follow-up study was conducted. The 3% who had written goals when they graduated in 1953 had a higher net worth than the other 97% of the class members combined! Think about that.

This success journal is where you can write down your dreams, hopes, and aspirations. This is where you can write your goals and the **action steps** it will take to accomplish them. Not anyone else's goals—your goals.

Grab a pen or pencil and on page 13 write down five things you want to have or accomplish in your life and why. If you have more than five goals—great! This is your journal, remember?

There are plenty of blank pages for you to write down as many dreams, goals, plans, and ideas as you want. So, find a blank page and write as much as you want to write. Here are a few things to keep in mind as you are writing:

✓ *Be sure to write down things that are important to YOU.* Write down what you love to do, what will make you happy, and what you are good at doing.

✓ *Write your goal in positive terms*. Saying, "I don't want to be broke" or "I hope I don't fail" are ineffective goals because those types of goals are based on fear and they keep you focused on negative events. You get more of what you focus on so, focus on success.

✓ *Make it clear and concrete.* Be specific about what you want. If you want a house or a car, what kind do you want? If you are going to travel around the world, what countries and cities are you going to visit or live in? If you want to be an entrepreneur, what kind of business will you start?

✓ *Think about now.* It's a good idea to have big dreams that will take time to accomplish, but you should also have goals and ideas that you can work on now. For example, having a goal of being the President of the United States is cool, but how about getting a better grade in history or a killer internship or job, first? It's better to spend most of your time working on short term goals that help you accomplish your big dreams and long term goals.

✓ **What's your yardstick?** Is your goal quantifiable? In other words, how do you know when you are making progress?

"What keeps me going is goals."

—Muhammad Ali, "The Greatest"

MY GOALS
(Hey! Remember to write down why each goal is important to you.)

1.

_____

_____

_____

_____

2.

_____

_____

_____

_____

3.

_____

_____

_____

_____

(There's room for more on the next page.)

"I have so many goals."
—Tyra Banks

4.

_____

_____

_____

_____

5.

_____

_____

_____

_____

MILLION-DOLLAR QUESTION:
Do you feel guilty about wanting any of your goals?

Take your time and seriously think about that.

Many people feel bad about wanting to have a lot of money because they think it's being greedy. (It's not. It's only greedy if you don't do anything good with your money. That's called being a Scrooge.)

If you feel guilty or ashamed about any of your goals then you need to talk to someone about them because you'll just be fighting against yourself. Talk to your best friend. Or maybe you can talk to your parents, a teacher, a counselor, your coach, or your mentor. If you need to, you can ask me about them. I'm easy to find. Just go to Facebook or Twitter and search for Al Duncan or go to my website: **www.DuncanNuggets.com** I answer questions from people just like you all the time.

Now take a few minutes to visualize yourself achieving each of your goals. Think about each one in detail and write down how you will feel and what accomplishing each one of your goals will mean to you.

HOW I WILL FEEL AND WHAT MY GOALS MEAN TO ME

1.

_____

_____

_____

2.

_____

_____

_____

3.

_____

_____

_____

_____

4.

_____

_____

_____

_____

5.

_____

_____

_____

_____

**First, have a definite, clear practical ideal;
a goal, an objective. Second, have
the necessary means to achieve
your ends; wisdom, money,
materials, and methods.
Third, adjust all your
means to that
end.**

—Aristotle

One of the main things that trips people up is, not knowing what it will take to accomplish their goals.

Think about the goals you've written down again. Now you're getting ready to write down what it is going to take to achieve them. Do you need a certain kind of degree? Do you need money? Maybe you need advice or mentoring.

If you're not sure exactly what it will take and what steps are necessary to get where you're going then do some research. Ask people you know, google your goals, buy a book or get it from the library, and like I said earlier if you need to, you can ask me. I'm easy to find. Just go to Facebook or Twitter and search for Al Duncan or go to my website: **www.DuncanNuggets.com** There's a place on the front page of my site where you can ask me questions.

Write down what it is going to take to achieve your goals. Be specific. If you don't know, find out. Write down at least one thing that you can do right now to start working on your goals.

STEPS FOR ACHIEVING MY GOALS

1.

_____

_____

_____

_____

2.

_____

_____

_____

_____

3.

_____

_____

_____

_____

4.

_____

_____

_____

_____

5.

_____

_____

_____

_____

_____

_____

_____

IT'S A JOURNEY, NOT A DESTINATION

Arthur Ashe, civil rights leader and the first African-American tennis player to win a Grand Slam event, offers this pearl of wisdom: **"Success is a journey, not a destination."** This journal, the free videos that go with it, and the articles and exercises in it are going to help you get started in the right direction. In fact, writing down your goals and what it is going to take to accomplish them is your first step in the right direction.

After the articles and exercises, there is plenty of room for you to write anything that you want to write about in your life. You can use your success journal to write down things you want to do, places you want go, and people you want to meet. But by all means, write and succeed.

"Thank God for the Journey."

—James Brown

HEY! Remember to check out the video for this chapter.
http://duncannuggets.com/success-journal-videos

3 things I learned in this chapter are...

_____

_____

_____

_____

_____

_____

One way I plan to use what I learned is...

_____

_____

_____

_____

_____

_____

_____

_____

Success is Personal

"I'm going to be successful!"

"I know you are. I believe that. So, what are you going to do?"

"I don't know, but I'm going to be a success."

"What's your definition of success?"

"Man, you know. I can't really put it into words, but that's what I'm gonna be."

—A conversation between Al Duncan and a graduate student

Success is a tricky word. Everybody has their own ideas about what it means to be successful. The challenging part for many people is that they are trying to live up to someone else's definition of success. Think about that for a minute.

Duncan Nugget® #7
If people tell you what success is and you blindly accept it, that's a problem because...*success is a personal choice.*

For example, let's look at the following question: Is getting an "A" on a test successful? The answer depends on your definition of success. You passed, of course, but is that the end? For me, passing a test is only small part of being successful. The real thing that I'm looking for is some knowledge that can help me be a better me. If I passed, but I didn't learn anything I wouldn't feel 100% satisfied. I wouldn't feel like a *complete* success. Maybe, you would think like me or maybe not. The point is: it's your choice.

THE MEANING OF SUCCESS

How many times have you seen or heard about someone working hard to get or accomplish something and when they succeeded, they weren't happy? Don't you know somebody who applied for a job, got it, and then hated it? What about thinking that some guy or girl is hot and then you find out that you don't really like him or her?

Most of the time, all of this happens because people are unclear about their personal definition of success so they ended up settling for less. You must determine what your definition of success is and be willing to work on it until you completely achieve it.

Do you want to be successful?

I've asked thousands and thousands of people, "do you want to be successful?" Nobody has ever said no. When I ask them "What does it take to be successful?" people have a ton of answers. With no hesitation, they say things like: hard work, dedication, perseverance, knowledge, and motivation.

But when I ask them, "What's your definition of success?" I get answers like: "Um..." or "That's a good question. I'm not sure." Quite often, I just get silence and a blank stare. That question leaves a lot of people scratching their heads because they aren't sure what success means to them. That's kind of crazy when you think about it.

Imagine this:

You ask me, "Where are you going"? I respond with, "I'm not really sure where I'm going, but I know how to get there." Would that make any sense? No!

MILLION-DOLLAR QUESTION:
How can you attain success if you don't even know what it is?

There isn't one specific way to become successful, but the process starts off with you clearly defining what success means to you.

Do you know what success is?

Write down your definition of success in the blanks on page 24. Remember, there's no right or wrong answer. This is YOUR definition of success. Here are a few things to keep in mind as you are writing:

✓ **What's the impact?** What are the consequences of your definition of success? Is it a definition that will make you AND other people better? Avoid definitions that are selfish and detrimental to you and others.

✓ **Things may change.** Your definition may change from time to time. That's okay as long as you know what your new definition is and why you want to make the change.

✓ **Avoid the extremes.** A young lady that I was mentoring once told me that she was only successful when she was the best at whatever she was doing. That's an ineffective definition because she has no control over the talent and abilities of other people. So, her definition of success can be discouraging and frustrating. It's more effective to think, "My *goal* is to be the best and as long as I'm getting better, I'm successful." She has more control over whether or not she is getting better. That's based on her personal effort.

✓ *Keep it positive*. Just like your goals, your definition of success should be positive. Saying, "As long as I don't screw up, I'm successful" is ineffective because that definition is based on fear and negativity. Create a definition that allows you to be positive and real with yourself.

✓ **Make sure it's fun *(sometimes)*.** Success requires work. You might not *always* like what you need to do, but most of the time your work should be enjoyable. Otherwise, you won't stick to it for long.

MY DEFINITION OF SUCCESS

_____

_____

_____

_____

_____

TIP: Now that you've written down what success means to you, go and find a picture that represents what you consider success to be and keep it in your journal. You might have to fold it up and that's okay. Just be sure to put it in your journal so that when life gets hard you can pull it out and look at it. Keep a rubber band around your success journal to keep your pictures or anything else from falling out.

A FINAL THOUGHT ABOUT SUCCESS

Everything we've just talked about has to do with your personal definition of success. Keep in mind, however, that teams and organizations have definitions of success as well.

If you choose to be part of a team or an organization make sure that their definition of success ultimately lines up with yours. The two definitions don't have to match exactly, but it can be very disheartening to be a part of a team or organization that doesn't help you to feel successful.

HEY! Remember to check out the video for this chapter.
http://duncannuggets.com/success-journal-videos

Duncan Nugget® #76:
Success is
not what you get,
it's what you become.

Duncan Nugget® #55:
Succes is
the right combination of
achievement and fulfillment.

Duncan Nugget® #133:
Success is
the reward of the diligent.

Duncan Nugget® #22:
Success is
only permanent
if you keep striving.

Duncan Nugget® #80:
Success is
what many crave, but
few can handle the
price to be paid.

is YOURS!

3 things I learned in this chapter are...

_____

_____

_____

_____

_____

_____

One way I plan to use what I learned is...

_____

_____

_____

_____

_____

_____

_____

Dealing with Failure

"But it's a struggle out here. You feel me? Life is hard. Sometimes my life's so hard that I'm like what's the point?"

"I feel you. At times life is crazy hard. So what? You think it'll be easier if you quit?"

"No, not really. But I'm sayin', I'm tryin' to do right, but I keep strugglin'?"

"Then you should realize that you're on your way to being successful."

"That don't sound right. How am I on my way to be a success when I feel like a failure?"

"Look, this is real talk, alright? You are exactly like all successful people. Everybody fails and everybody has felt like a failure, but failure is only permanent if you quit."

"True...true. I'm feelin' that. Hit me wit' some more o' dat knowledge."

—A conversation between Al Duncan and a teenage gang member

If you are absolutely, positively determined to be successful, then at some point in time, it's practically guaranteed that you will experience failure and some type of fear. Dealing with failure and conquering fear are two of the vital keys to success. We'll talk about fear in the next chapter.

DEALING WITH FAILURE

People will lecture you all day long about failure. They say things like, "it's not the end of the world", "at least you did your best", and "if at first you don't succeed, try, try again." Those statements are true. What they don't teach you, however, is *how to get better at dealing with failure.* Having your goals written down, visualizing them, and clearly defining success are of little use without the ability to bounce back from failure.

There is good failure (known as failing forward) and bad failure (known as failing backwards). The difference between the two is that when you fail forward, you get knowledge and skills that you didn't have and you avoid repeating the mistake. This requires grit , resilience and the ability to identify and master the lesson to be learned.

Grit is passion and perseverance in pursuit of a long term goal. Resilience is the ability to recover quickly from what you have endured. In terms of dealing with failure, you will have more grit and resilience as well as a better chance of failing forward when you:

1. **Focus on your goals and why they are important to you.** Constantly reflecting on your goals, why you want them, and what it will feel like to achieve them will give you strength when you need it.

2. **Understand that "this too, shall pass."** Failure never feels good, but you get over it faster with experience.

3. **Realize that nothing can keep you down for long.** Every time you experience failure, successfully deal with it, and then succeed, your self-confidence grows. You begin to feel and act like the unstoppable force that you are.

4. **Know that failure has nothing to do with your value as a person.** You (not anything or anyone else) determine how much you are worth. Self-worth is a state of mind.

5. **Have a reliable Circle of Wisdom.** Every successful person has a least one person they can talk to or call on for help. It could be a parent, mentor, coach, counselor, teacher, or professor. It could be a pastor, priest, minister, rabbi, imam, or spiritual advisor. And of course, it could be your close friend.

WARNING: Be careful about who you go to for support and advice. Make sure he/she knows what he/she is talking about and be sure that he/she has your best interest in mind.

(Complete the phrase.)
To me, the difference between failing foward and failing backwards is...

_____

_____

_____

MASTER THE LESSON

Without failure and struggle there are certain lessons that could never be learned. If you find that you fail at or struggle with the same things over and over again, then you haven't mastered the lesson. If you can't identify and master your lesson then you are bound to repeat your failure until you do. It's as simple and as complicated as that.

"If there is no struggle, there is no progress."
—Frederick Douglass

In the world of physical fitness, there is a theory called *The Overload Principle*. In a nutshell, it states that, within reason, the body will adapt to the stresses placed upon it. So, if you lift weights you will get stronger. If you do aerobics, which is good for your cardiovascular system, your stamina will increase.

Back in the day, the older folks didn't call it *The Overload Principle*. They simply said, *"If it doesn't kill ya, it'll make ya stronger."* That phrase should end with: *"if you identify and master the lesson."*

Identifying and mastering each lesson that accompanies failure is mental weight lifting and aerobics for the mind. You will get mentally stronger and sharper by thoroughly analyzing each failure in order to identify and eventually master your lesson.

Going through the same old struggles time and time again is frustrating. It can seriously drain your self-confidence, self-worth, self-esteem, and self-motivation as well your sense of autonomy and competence. It could cause you to think things like, "What's the point? There's nothing that I can do about this." There are times when that statement is true because certain things are out of your control. But nine times out of ten, if you put your mind to it, there is *something* that you can do—master the lesson, which will give you the self-confidence and fortitude necessary for future struggles and failures.

There are different types of lessons. Some are easy to recognize and hard to master, while others are hard to pinpoint, but not as challenging to learn. In many cases, correctly identifying the lesson can be the most difficult part of the process, especially if you think you did everything right.

So, let's work on identifying and mastering your lessons. Below, you will find space to write down a recent problem, situation, or failure you experienced or something with which you are currently struggling. Next, work on identifying the lesson and finally, write down what you can do right now to start mastering your lesson. Here are a few things to keep in mind as you are writing:

- ✓ **Use Al as a guinea pig.** If you can't think of anything, you are welcome to use my failures for practice. A few of them are listed on the next page.

- ✓ **A little help might be nice.** If you are having a hard time putting your finger on an elusive lesson, you may need some help. This is an ideal time to call on your Circle of Wisdom. Remember... "The smart man learns from his mistakes, but the wise man learns from the mistakes of others."

- ✓ **You might need a professional.** If you are struggling with your new business, your health, mental problems, or if you are extremely depressed it would be more advantageous to get professional help. If you need to, you can ask me about it. Just go to Facebook or Twitter and search for Al Duncan or check out my website: **www.DuncanNuggets.com**

- ✓ **Get knowlege. Develop skills.** When you master the lesson, you gain knowledge and develop skills that will enable you to avoid making the same or similar mistakes in the future. Your mission: *Master the lesson.*

A RECENT FAILURE AND THE LESSON(S) LEARNED

_____

_____

_____

Al Duncan's Failures

I've failed so many times that I feed on failure. It makes me stronger. Here are a FEW of the times I've experienced failure and humiliation:

☹ I've been in the top 5% of my class. Two years later I was in the bottom 5% of my class.

☹ As a professional musician, I've been on stage playing my saxophone in front of thousands of people and completely forgot the song I was supposed to be playing.

☹ I played myself by calling somebody the wrong name twice in one day. (It was my girlfriend!)

☹ Once I forgot what I was to going to say in a speech. I was standing in front of over two-thousand people.

☹ Somebody pulled down my shorts in front of the entire class during gym!

☹ The first time I took the SAT I didn't even score a thousand. (Don't worry, I killed it the second time.)

☹ When I was 22, I was arrested because I was hanging out with the wrong people. (No convictions and all charges were dropped. Thank God!)

☹ I've nearly been bankrupt three times. (That's how life is for many entrepreneurs and musicians.)

☹ I've been evicted twice and been homeless once. (It was my fault.)

☹ I've been sued for not paying a bill on time.

☹ I had the worst basketball game of my life in front of my entire high school. I had no points, 6 or 7 rebounds, and at least 9 turnovers. (I handled my biz next game, but everybody kept talking about the other game.)

☹ When I was a chef, one time I accidentally burned up all the food for a banquet for 500 people. (Can you say FIRED?!)

**But none of that could stop me.
Today I am a successful entrepreneur,
the author of 4 books (more on the way...), and
one of the top speakers in the world for young people.**

**And what ever struggles you go through
can't stop you either.**

Duncan Nugget® #21
Failure is only permanent if you quit.

YOUR DECLARATION TO LEARN FROM FAILURE

Here's a bonus tip for dealing with failure: Quite often, when people experience failure the things they say to themselves are worse then anything the people are around them are saying. Think about that. Have you ever called yourself stupid? If you're like most people you have. As matter of fact, to keep it real, I've even cursed myself out! Do you know anybody else who has done that? You would probably want to fight if anyone else said some of things to you that you say to yourself.

It's nothing wrong with pushing yourself and demanding the best, but beating yourself up isn't productive or helpful. So, what are some good things to say when you're dealing with failure? It can be hard to find the right words to say. In fact, it might be easier if you plan something out ahead of time. A declaration can be a powerful tool for dealing with failure.

To "make a declaration" means "to state an official intention to undertake a particular course of action or adopt a particular status." So, right now you are going to create a declaration. Your declaration will convey the actions you will take and the mindset you will adopt when experiencing failure. On the next page you will find a template for your *Declaration to Learn from Failure*. Here are some things to keep in mind as you are working on your declaration:

✓ Wherever you see a blank in the template, you can insert any word or phrase that comes to mind.

✓ On pages 34 to 36 you will see five groups of words. (Please excuse my handwriting!) Each group is represented by a letter. In the blank spaces of your declaration you will see the letter of a group. If you are having trouble thinking of a word or phrase you can choose any word from the matching group and use it to fill in the blank.

✓ You can change up the template if you want to. You can find a blank page in your success journal and write your own *Declaration to Learn from Failure*.

✓ Whenever you experience failure, stand in front of a mirror and read your declaration out loud at least 3 times.

MY DECLARATION TO LEARN FROM FAILURE

Failure is something that all successful people experience and because I make every effort to be successful, sooner or later I will experience failure. When I do, I will be even more **(A)**_____ on my road to success because failure is only permanent if I quit.

When I feel down, frustrated, and discouraged, it's time to **(B)**_____ and understand that there is always a lesson to be learned from failure. I will recognize and master that lesson.

Failure cannot stop me. Only I can stop me and I am too **(C)**_____ to be stopped. So, I strive for greatness, but I remain humble and willing to grow.

Like all **(D)**_____, step by step I will earn my place amongst the successful because **(E)**_____.

Had I known better, I would've done better. Now I know better, so I'll do better. I will succeed.

_____
(Signature and date)

A

determined undaunted steady
vigilant courageous
steadfast unstoppable
unwavering focused
diligent

B

Man up! take action ~~cry~~
get busy talk to my BFF
shake it off overcome fight back
regroup stop crying stop complaining
pick myself up talk to my mentor get better
keep my eye on the prize Suck it up
get focused remember my goal
be strong rise up get tough

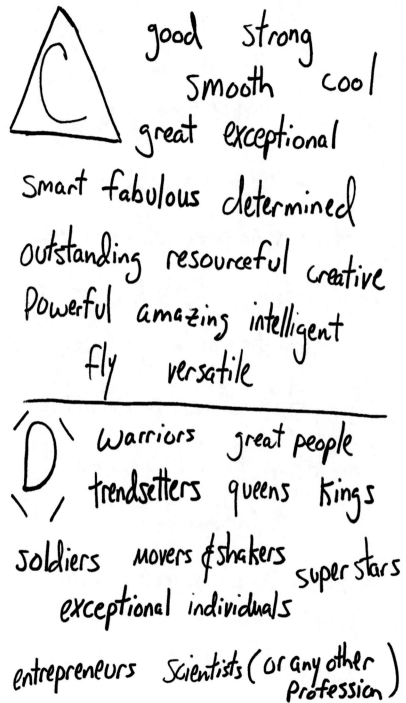

good strong
smooth cool
great exceptional
smart fabulous determined
outstanding resourceful creative
powerful amazing intelligent
fly versatile

warriors great people
trendsetters queens kings
soldiers movers & shakers super stars
exceptional individuals
entrepreneurs scientists (or any other profession)

it's my destiny.
success is non-negotiable.
I'm fired up & ready to go!

that's my swag. I said so.
there is no other option for me.

it's my future. that's how I roll.
I'm destined for greatness.

that's my style. I want the best in life.
it's my legacy. that's how we do it.

I believe in me!

that's what I'm supposed to do.
people are depending on me.

anything less would be uncivilized.

I've missed more than 9000 shots in my career.
I've lost almost 300 games. 26 times,
I've been trusted to take the game
winning shot and missed. I've
failed over and over and
over again in my life.
And that is why
I succeed.

Michael Jordan

HEY! Remember to check out the video for this chapter.
http://duncannuggets.com/success-journal-videos

3 things I learned in this chapter are...

_____

_____

_____

_____

_____

_____

One way I plan to use what I learned is...

_____

_____

_____

_____

_____

_____

_____

_____

Conquer Fear

"I ain't afraid of nothin'."

"Are you sure? Everybody gets at least a little bit nervous about something."

"Not me."

"Do you mean to tell me that nothing worries you or makes you nervous?"

"Bro', I'm telling you. I ain't scared of nothin'. Snakes, alligators, people, guns, or whatever. I ain't even scarred of dyin'."

"Cool. Here's my introduction. I need you to go up on stage and read it to everybody."

"Man, are you crazy?! I can't get up there in front of all those people like that."

—A conversation between Al Duncan and a college student
before a speaking engagement

Fear is one the most powerful forces governing our behavior. It is the feeling of being threatened by something physically (a gun), mentally (a test), or emotionally (he might leave me). Regardless of whether the threat is real (a hungry bear) or imagined (what if everybody laughs at me?) your body initially responds the same way—you go into *Flight-or-Fight Response.*

When your body fears for its physical, mental, or emotional safety it decides that action is required. It's time run or rumble. If somebody yells, "watch out!" it is fear that causes you to move out of the way just in time. Without fear, the piano that they were moving probably would've landed on your head instead of on the ground.

As you can probably tell, the purpose of fear and *Flight-or-Fight Response* is to protect you from harm. This means that fear, like all emotions, starts with good intentions. But have you ever heard the expression *"the road to hell is paved with good intentions"*? You can put yourself through hell if you allow your fear to run amuck. Untamed fear will wreak havoc on dreams, goals, plans, and ideas. Fear, unconquered, can erode self-confidence, self-worth, self-esteem, and self-motivation. So, if you want to be successful, your fear must be identified and conquered.

A lot of people are like me. I get nervous, but I don't *show* that I'm nervous. Where I come from (North Philly), it's not cool to show fear. It's considered to be a sign of weakness. They say it makes you look like a punk, a chump, or a coward. Maybe you agree with all of that, maybe you don't, but one thing is for sure—being nervous or afraid is NOT the sign of a coward.

The hero and the coward both feel the same thing, but the hero uses his fear, projects it onto his opponent, while the coward runs. It's the same thing, fear, but it's what you do with it that matters.

—*Cus D'Amato*
(Boxing Trainer)

That pearl of wisdom you just read is called *The Lesson of the Hero and the Coward* and the message is simple: You have to refuse allow fear, especially the fear of failure, to keep you from accomplishing your goals and being successful. It's okay to be nervous, apprehensive, or even afraid as long as you do what have to do. (And let's keep it legal, okay?)

Duncan Nugget® #163
The difference between a hero
and a coward is not the lack of fear,
it's the lack of action.

WERE YOU BORN SCARED?

You and everybody else on this planet—from the bravest, hardcore warriors to the weakest, spineless cowards—were only born with two fears. Any other type of fear is a learned behavior.

Out of all the different fears that humans have which are the two that everybody is born with? *(The answer is at the bottom of page 42.)*

It's not always easy to identify your fears, but it is beneficial because there's a good chance that some type of fear is blocking your success and keeping you from attaining your goals.

Some things are obvious. If you start screaming whenever you see a mouse, it's safe to say that you're afraid of mice. But when a person is reluctant to stand in the front of the room and talk about the project that he or she has been diligently working on, it could be for a number of different reasons:

✓ ***Is it the fear of failure or public speaking?***
("Man, are you crazy?! I can't get up there in front of all of those people like that.")

✓ ***Is the fear of success or responsibility?***
("If I do this and they like it, they are going to want me to be project manger. I don't want that headache.")

✓ ***Is it the fear of embarrassment or ridicule?***
("I know I'm a good presenter, but what if they don't like my idea? What if they don't like my outfit? What if they don't like me?!")

You probably realize that it could be a combination of all of those fears so, how do you figure this out? What's one of the keys to conquering your fears? You have to identify what makes you nervous, worried, or afraid. One the best ways to do this is to write about it in your success journal.

It's not always easy to talk or write about your fears so, I'll go first. The main fears I've wrestled with over the last ten years are on the next page.

"Named must your fear be before banish it you can."
—Yoda
(Jedi Master from the Star Wars movies)

I'm afraid of:

1. **Not reaching my full potential.** My #1 fear by far. This is a form of the fear of failure. Can you believe that I've even had nightmares about this? Being mediocre...I don't even want to think about it. This fear started when I realized how much of my time and potential I wasted.

   Status: CONQUERED

2. **Something happening to my family and not being able to do anything about it.** I've probably been watching too many movies! But seriously, I've seen some insane things growing up in North Philly. This is the fear of feeling helpless and the fear of loss.

   Status: CONQUERED

3. **Natural disasters.** This is another example of the fear of feeling helpless. I don't do hurricanes, earthquakes, or anything like them. Just the thought of moving to Miami or California makes me nervous. (But I will definitely go anywhere on the planet for a speaking engagement.)

   Status: CONQUERED

4. **Drowning.** Maybe I should learn how swim a little bit better. I'm not scared of the water, but drowning...or getting eaten by sharks I can't handle.

   Status: I'M WORKING ON IT!

You were only born with two fears: the fear of loud noises & the fear of falling

NAME THAT FEAR

Now it's your turn. On the next page, write down your fears. Here are a few things to keep in mind as you are writing:

✓ **Types of fear.** If you are having a hard time thinking of different types of fear, I've listed some common ones on page 45 to help you get started.

✓ **Keep your ego in check.** Be careful if you're sitting here thinking, "I'm not afraid of anything." Even if you're not "afraid" of anything, there are probably some things that make you nervous. You have to identify what these things are because you may be unconsciously avoiding actions you need to take due to some hidden fears.

✓ **Cover the different types.** Be sure to write a combination of fears that are based on feeling threatened physically, mentally, or emotionally.

✓ **Watch for the roadblocks.** Take special note of the ones that are blocking your success or keeping you from taking action on your goals. Write down one thing you can to do to help yourself conquer that fear. If you don't know, ask someone.

✓ **When to get help.** If your fear is so extreme that you have panic attacks, experience dizziness, get light headed, or feint, then you might have a phobia. Phobias, such as claustrophobia (the fear of enclosed spaces), are the most common type of anxiety disorder. It might be beneficial to get some professional advice if you have a phobia that's affecting your life on a daily basis.

"How you get so fly? From not being afraid to fall out the sky..."
—Jay Z

QUESTIONS FOR WORKING ON YOUR FEAR(S)
(Remember, starting on page 63, there are plenty of blank pages if you need them.)

1. **Am I nervous about this?** If yes, what is it about this situation that's causing me to feel nervous? How will I deal with what's causing me to feel nervous?

2. **Am I worried about this?** If yes, what is it about this situation that's causing me to worry? How will I deal with what's causing me to worry?

3. **Am I afraid?** If yes, then exactly what am I afraid of? How will I conquer it?

By the way, do you realize that some people are even afraid to admit that they're afraid or nervous? Think about that.

"Don't be scurred."
—Ludacris

MY FEAR(S) OR WHAT MAKES ME NERVOUS AND HOW I WILL CONQUER IT

_____

_____

_____

_____

_____

_____

_____

Types of Fear

Heights

Flying

fear of the hurt

fear of the unknown

Mice

fear of ridicule

fear of public speaking

fear of embarrassment

fear of death

fear of crowds

fear of loss

fear of failure

fear of

fear of

fear of

People

Stage fright

fear of success

fear of commitment

fear of responsibility

fear of abandonment

Snakes

Spiders

Fear of rejection

Fear of messing up

Fear of change

Fear of feeling Helpless

3 things I learned in this chapter are...

_____

_____

_____

_____

_____

One way I plan to use what I learned is...

_____

_____

_____

_____

_____

_____

_____

What's Your Brand?

"Hey! Why is my medicine so expensive this time? It's usually a lot cheaper than this. What's up with that?"

"Mr. Duncan, you normally get generics, but your doctor instructed us to give you the name brand medicine this time."

"Does it do anything different? I mean, it costs twice as much. Is it twice as good?"

"Not really, it's just the fact that it's name brand. The brand is what you're paying for."

—A conversation between Al Duncan and the pharmacist

If I asked you to think of your favorite place to shop, different images and words would immediately begin popping into your head. I could also ask you to think about any company or successful person you know and once again images and words would immediately come to mind. Those words and images aren't popping into your head by accident.

Successful people, companies, and organizations spend a great deal of time, energy, and resources (that includes money) to make sure that people are thinking certain things about them. They want people to think these things so that they will associate or do business with them. This is known as branding. A brand is a symbolic embodiment of all the information connected to a company, product, service, or individual.

Duncan Nugget® #71
Your personal brand is a representation
of YOU in the minds of other people.
It is the perception people have
about your character as well as
the quality and value of
what you do.

If you never thought about or worked on your personal brand, now is a good time to get started because it plays a major part in your journey to success. Your personal brand could be the difference between you getting the internship, scholarship, job, or promotion instead of someone else getting it. If you are an entrepreneur, your personal brand has a huge impact on whether or not someone will do business with you. Your personal brand could even be the difference between you getting a date or not! (Who wants to go out with someone whose brand is *"lame"*?)

So, let's work on your personal brand right now. You're going to create your personal brand declaration. This is similar to what you did in the chapter on failure. Below you will find 9 questions. On page 50 there is a template for your declaration. Wherever you see a blank for your name, put your name (duh!). The other blanks are numbered 1-9. Put the answer to the questions in the blanks with the same number. Here are a few things to keep in mind as you are writing:

✓ **It's a personal choice.** There are no right or wrong answers to these questions.

✓ **Keep it professional.** Don't be silly. Stick to answers that will help you achieve your goals. I know you want to be the coolest person ever, but trust me—I know from personal experience—being paid and successful is very cool.

✓ **It's not permanent**. Your brand doesn't have to be written in stone. You may want to change things down the road and that's okay.

✓ **Keep it real.** Seriously. Just be yourself. It's okay to put down things you are striving for, but don't be a faker.

✓ **Have fun.** Chillax. I know a lot is riding on your brand, but that doesn't mean that this has to be a pain in the butt. Well...at least not all of the time.

QUESTIONS FOR BUILDING YOUR PERSONAL BRAND

1. What is one thing you are passionate about?

_____

2. What is one thing will you do in life or die trying? (Keep it legal!)

_____

3. What special qualities do you look for in a friend?

_____

4. What do you like most about your character?

_____

5. What is your greatest gift to the world?

_____

6. If you could have any type of career you want, what would it be? (If you want to own a business, write "entrepreneur".)

_____

7. What is the one thing you would do if you were 100% guaranteed to succeed?

_____

8. In terms of your career and being successful, what is your greatest fear?

_____

9. In one positive, professional word, how would you describe be yourself?

_____

MY PERSONAL BRAND DECLARATION

My name is _____ and I am a person of value who is passionate about (1)_____
_____.

When I walk into a room, people will know that there is something special about me because my life has meaning and my personal brand is clear.

I am determined to (2)_____
_____ and NOTHING will stop me.

When it comes to others, I look for people who will enhance my life because they are (3)_____.

When it comes to me, I will let my (4)_____ shine through. I am valuable because of who I am. As part of my legacy, I will give (5) _____ to the world.

Today, I have decided to achieve my goal of becoming a (6)_____. But I reserve the right to change my mind because I am committed to having a career that I am passionate about. I have the tenacity and the audacity to (7)_____ if I so desire.

I will confront and conquer my fear of (8)_____
_____. I will use that and all of my other fears as fuel to make me stronger and propel me towards my dreams. I am committed to living a life that I love while having a positive impact on the world.

BrandTastrophe:
3 Things That Could
Destroy Your Brand

"Hey...hey...why are you crying like that?"

"M...m...Mr. Duncan. They...they...took my scholarship!"

"What?! Who took your scholarship?"

"The scholarship committee. They t...t...took it back."

"What happened?!"

"I accepted a friend request, but...but...I didn't know she was from the scholarship committee. They looked at all of my pictures and notes and said it didn't match what I wrote on my essay."

—A conversation between Al Duncan and a high school senior who lost a $25,000/yr. full scholarship because of her Facebook page

I. Social Media

Wow. A $100,000 scholarship lost because of something on Facebook. That's what I call a brand catastrophe or *BrandTastrophe*. Things like that happen all the time. In fact, nowadays it seems like everybody and their grandmas have an account on Facebook, Twitter, or some other social media site. There's nothing wrong with social media. (I'm on Facebook and Twitter. I even have a Facebook Fan Page.) Most social media sites can help you build your brand. They give people a chance to connect with you and learn more about you. That can be helpful when you're trying to get a job, internship, scholarship, or get into college.

If you are not careful, however, Facebook and other social media sites can cause a BrandTastrophe. They will eat up all of your time, ruin your reputation, and cost you money.

THE LEGEND OF CISCO FATTY

Imagine that you are 22 years old. You get a job offer from Cisco, one of the largest companies in the world, and you head off to Twitter to tweet your thoughts:

"Cisco just offered me a job! Now I have to weigh the utility of a fatty paycheck against the daily commute to San Jose and hating the work."

Someone claiming to be a Cisco employee responds to your tweet:

"Who is the hiring manager? I'm sure they would love to know that you will hate the work. We here at Cisco are versed in the Web."

In a matter of hours, thousands of people are writing about you all over the internet and as a result, you lose the job offer. Now people are calling you an idiot for wasting a good job opportunity. Newspapers pick up the story and TV shows even start to talk about you. When someone *googles* your name he finds thousands of links to information about what you did. So, you are having a hard time getting a new job because when employers do a search on you, they see all of the stories about what you posted on Twitter. Ouch.

This is a nightmare—especially if your name is Connor Riley. On the internet Connor Riley is known as Cisco Fatty.

TRICK OR TREAT, YOU'RE FIRED!

In October 2008, Kevin Colvin was interning at a bank. He emailed his boss, Paul Davis, late in the day on Halloween to let him know that he wasn't going to make it to work for the next few days. He had a family emergency in New York. The next day Paul read the email. He also checked Kevin's Facebook page. He found a picture of Kevin at a Halloween party wearing a Tinkerbell costume while holding a magic wand in one hand and a can of beer in the other. (Busted!) There was no family emergency. Kevin just wanted a couple of days off after partying so hard.

Paul sent the following email, with the Tinkerbell photo in it, to

Kevin and everybody else at the office:

"Thanks for letting me know—hope everything is OK in New York. (cool wand)"

Fired! And the story about Kevin Colvin and his Tinkerbell picture is all over the internet—forever.

YOUR FIRST DAY IS YOUR LAST DAY

Recently, I saw a CNN clip on YouTube about Kimberly Swann. During her first day on a new job, Kimberly, a 16-year old girl, updated her Facebook status:

"first day at work. omg!! So dull!!"

Her boss saw her status and the next thing you know...

Fired!

Picture yourself trying to explain to the person interviewing that you were fired on your first day of work. Not cool. Kimberly Swann has had to explain that story many times. Why? Because if you Google her name that's the first story that comes up. *omg!!*

ANYTHING YOU POST CAN AND WILL BE USED AGAINST YOU

It was total chaos. People were setting fires, throwing rocks, smashing windows, and causing all kinds of damage. Police showed up, started arresting people, and began to restore order on the campus of the University of Massachusetts. Many of the students who participated in the riot on December 15th, 2006, ran before the police arrived. But within several months, 57 people—most of them students—were arrested and charged with various acts of violence.

How did they catch them? What did they use for evidence? They used pictures and videos that students in the riot posted on MySpace, Facebook, and YouTube.

How mad would you be if you couldn't pass a background check because of a video or picture posted online?

THE POINT IS...

There are thousands of stories like the ones you just read. That's ridiculous. Too many young people have serious problems that are the result of something posted online. Here are 7 nuggets that will keep you from ending up like Cisco Fatty, Kevin Colvin, or Kimberly Swann.

7 Nuggets to Remember About Social Media

1. **Never post anything online that could keep you from getting into college or keeping a job, internship, or scholarship.** Even if your page is set to "private" be careful. If it's online there is always a possibility that something you don't want the world to see could end up in the wrong hands.

2. **Never post anything that proves you did something illegal. (How about just not doing anything illegal?)** If you're not sure whether or not something could get you jammed up then don't post it.

3. **Do not harass, threaten, or bully people online (or anywhere else).** It can get you kicked out of school, fired, arrested, or all of the above.

4. **It would really suck to have a BrandTastrophe because of something you didn't even post.** Set your Facebook page to send you a text when someone writes on your wall or tags you in a picture or video. And if someone does tag you in something inappropriate it might be time to unfriend him or her.

5. **Be picky about who you accept as a friend.** (Duh!)

6. **Even if you're the head of some secret government agency, you pretty much have zero chance of stopping anything that goes viral.** It is extremely difficult (maybe even impossible) to get things taken off of the internet once the story starts to spread.

7. **If there is something crazy posted about you on the internet your story could end up on the news or in my next book!** Real talk—I will write about you. But...I'll still love you!

II. Your Email Address

"Delete...delete..."

For about three minutes straight that's all I heard from a good friend of mine. She is responsible for deciding who get's an interview for a job with the company she works for.

"Delete...delete...delete..."

My friend is an HR Director. I'm not going to say her name because I'm not sure if what she does is okay with the company. You might not even think that what she does is fair. One thing, however, is for sure—it might not be right, but it's real.

My friend was deleting job applicants that have crazy, stupid, and vulgar email addresses. She's not the only person who does this. Everyday people loose out on opportunities to get scholarships, internships, and jobs because of inappropriate email addresses.

Million-Dollar Question:
What does your
email address say about you?

Here are three crazy email addresses that I saw recently. (They emailed me asking about internships.):

qtpie09@****.com

shawdymac@****.com

getdatcash@****.com

I emailed the students back and explained to them that it's not cool to use your "cool" email address when emailing people for professional reasons. Hopefully, they listened. If they did, they got off easy because a lot of professionals would just click "delete" without responding.

How many email addresses can YOU have?

As many as you want—most of them are free. Make sure one of your email addresses is professional sounding and use that address whenever you email a college, company, or a professional contact. Here are three professional sounding email addresses that I've seen recently:

al@duncannuggets.com

jbrown@****.com

traceylewis11@****.com

How mad would you be if you found the perfect opportunity, but you couldn't take advantage of it because of your email address?

4 Nuggets to Remember
About Your Email Address

1. **Unless you are emailing a friend or family member, use a professional sounding email address.** No exceptions.

2. **If you have used a crazy sounding email address in the past and gotten away with it you're lucky.** But don't try it again.

3. **If you are applying for or asking about a job, college, internship, or scholarship, proofread your email.** (Duh!)

4. **If you ever think about sending an email to a college or a company from your cool email address, remember this:** "Delete."

III. Your Cell Phone

If you put your cell phone number on an application, what's going to happen? Somebody is going to call you. And when she calls you, what does she hear? She hears your ring back tone (if you have one) and your voice mail greeting. Think about that.

If someone is calling you about a job, internship, scholarship, or getting into college, she does not want to hear your two minute long voice mail.

Remember my friend *"Delete"* that you read about earlier? She told me that in addition to the crazy email addresses, she also deletes job applicants with inappropriate ring back tones and ridiculous sounding voice mail greetings.

How mad would you be if you are the best person for the job, internship, college, or scholarship, but you don't get it because of your ring back tone or voice mail greeting?

If you just have to have your ring back tone and cool sounding voice mail then use a different phone number on your application. Otherwise, turn off the ring back tone and record a short and professional sounding voice mail greeting. You can change things back after you get whatever you've applied for.

ALL EYES ON YOU

Camera and video phones can get you seriously jammed up. Lots of celebrities, athletes, professionals, and students have been caught in pictures and videos doing stupid or illegal stuff. Haven't you seen pictures and videos online of famous and not-so-famous people doing dumb things? Make sure you're not one of them.

Everybody has messed up before (I have done too many stupid things to count), but technology has completely changed the game. You won't catch me doing anything stupid anymore because in a matter of minutes the whole world could know. (Also, I've learned from those stupid things. What's worse than doing something stupid is doing the same stupid things over and over again.)

There's no need to be paranoid. Still have fun, but be smart about it, okay?

THINK and pay attention.

THE TRAGEDY OF A NAKED PICTURE

Jessie Logan made a mistake—a HUGE mistake. She took a naked picture of herself with her camera phone and sent it to her boyfriend. When the two broke up, he sent the naked picture of Jessie to the entire school. (That guy is lame.)

People in the school sent it to people in other schools and soon thousands of people in her school district had the photo. Everybody was teasing and harassing her. They said nasty stuff when they saw her and sent her vulgar text messages. Her rep was ruined. It was torture.

Jessie was a graduating senior in high school when all of this happened and she hoped it would go away after graduation. It didn't. People everywhere were still harassing her and it got worse. Finally, Jessie couldn't take it anymore and she committed suicide.

The story of Jessie Logan has been shown on hundreds of news shows and it's all over YouTube. It's a tragic example of what a dangerous game sexting can be.

I'm only going to say one thing about sexting. If you send someone a naked picture of yourself or if you send people naked pictures of someone else you are taking a serious risk. It could ruin you.

In some states it's illegal and you could face criminal charges. The pictures (and the story about what happened) could end up online and when someone goes to Google or Google Images to do a search on you, they will find the naked pictures—forever.

6 Nuggets to Remember
About Your Cell Phone

1. **If you're waiting to hear from someone about a job, internship, scholarship, or getting into college, turn off your ring back tone.** You can always turn it back on later after you get hired or accepted.

2. **If you're waiting to hear from someone about a**

job, internship, scholarship, or getting into college, make sure that your voice mail greeting is short and professional. If you feel like you need to sing or talk all sexy or whatever on your voice mail, do it after you get hired or accepted.

3. **Real talk—turn off the ring back tone.** Seriously, at least turn it off until you are accepted or hired.

4. **Set up your voicemail.** I've called dozens of students about all kinds of opportunities and I couldn't leave them a message because their mail box was full or it wasn't even set up in the first place. Grr... That's really irritating!

5. **Be respectful with your camera and video phone.** Everybody doesn't want their picture taken. Keep an eye out for people taking pictures or videos of you in weird situations.

6. **Sexting is a dangerous game.** It could ruin you.

Social media, your email address, and your cell phone aren't good or bad. They're just tools. Whether or not they cause a BrandTastrophe is up to you. It has nothing to with grades or ability. It's all about the most important part of your personal brand—character and reputation.

Duncan Nugget® #58
Your character and reputation
will build or destroy your personal brand.

BONUS TIPS FOR BUILDING YOUR BRAND ONLINE

1. **A few times per month, google yourself.** More and more colleges and companies are googling people. Keep a constant eye on the information about you.

2. **Make sure they can find something.** A few years ago when people googled you, if nothing came up that was okay, but now that's not always good. Somebody who is trying to get the same job, internship, scholarship, or college acceptance letter that you are, probably has something good posted about him on Google.

You should, too. It could be an article or note written by you or about you. Or maybe it could be a blog post or your personal website.

3. **Get your domain name.** If you can, go buy [*yourname*].com or [*yourname*].net (People, including me, have started buying the domain names for their kids as soon as they are born!) If someone already has [*yourname*].com or .net then use your middle name or initial as part of your domain name. **Actually, most of the time you should be using your middle initial anyway.** It separates you from people with the same name, especially famous people with the same name.

4. **Take control of your Google Profile.** Go to Google and sign up for an account if you don't have one. Then set up your Google Profile. Make it professional (use info that will help you get hired or accepted) and use a good photo. When someone Googles you, your Google profile will show up at the bottom of the fist page with your photo next to it. When they click through they will be able to check out your profile. That's an easy way to make sure people are seeing some good things about you online.

Duncan Nugget® #56
In today's highly competitive market, it is important to be able to distinguish yourself by developing Brand YOU.

Million-Dollar Question:
What are you doing to differentiate yourself from your competition?

HEY! Remember to check out the video for this chapter. http://duncannuggets.com/success-journal-videos

Your Personal GPS

> "Hey. Can you help me figure out where I am going? I've been driving around forever. I'm trying to get to the university, but the directions I printed out are wrong."
>
> "I would love to help you out, but I'm not at my computer right now."
>
> "Aw, man! This is seriously messed up. I've got to get to my gig and nobody around here knows how to get to the school."
>
> "You know, you wouldn't be having this problem if you had..."
>
> "Yeah, yeah, I know...if I had GPS."
>
> —A telephone conversation between Al Duncan and a friend
> 30 minutes before a speaking engagement

Everything that you've been learning and writing in your success journal up to this point is helping you to create your personal **GPS**. Normally, GPS stands for Global Positioning System. It's a great little gadget that pinpoints exactly where you—or any object equipped with it—are and it can guide you to your destination. (Yes, I do have GPS on my phone. That story happened when GPS first came out.)

In terms of success, GPS stands for **Guiding Principles for Success.** As you've been working your way through your success journal you've been designing your GPS. Now that you are headed in the right direction it's time for you to take control of the navigation system and if you ever start getting off track it's your GPS that will guide you back.

After this chapter, there are plenty of blank pages for you to write whatever you want to write, but at the top of every other page there is a daily pharse for you to complete. I'm expecting you to do these. Not because you owe me anything—I expect you to do them because you owe it to yourself. You have just as much right as anybody else to be successful **if you do the work.**

Also, you will notice that throughout the rest of your success journal there are more *Duncan Nuggets®*—short articles, quotes, tips, and action steps that you can add to your GPS to help you stay on course.

WHAT TO WRITE

If you are not sure what to write, here are some suggestions:

✓ New goals that you want to achieve.

✓ Song lyrics and quotes that inspire you.

✓ Ideas that you want to work on.

✓ Places you want to visit.

✓ Schools you want to attend and degrees you want to acquire.

✓ Notes from a seminar, sermon, or workshop. (You should take notes whenever you go to these types of events. *"A short pencil beats a long memory every time."*)

✓ Your accomplishments and how you plan to celebrate your success.

✓ Your frustrations or disappointments and how you will deal with them.

✓ ANYTHING else that you learn that you want to add to your **GPS.**

As I've said several times already, if you have some questions, I'm easy to find. Just go to Facebook or Twitter and search for Al Duncan or go to my website: **www.DuncanNuggets.com** I wish you all the best, much success, and happiness. Until next time, may you be safe, be well, and be blessed.

Duncan Nugget® #1:
Write and succeed.
Writing down what you want and how you plan to get it is crucial to your success. You are far more likely to do what it takes to achieve your dreams, goals, and aspirations if you plan it out in writing.

3 things I learned in this chapter are...

_____

_____

_____

_____

_____

_____

One way I plan to use what I learned is...

_____

_____

_____

_____

_____

_____

_____

_____

Today is a great day to...

_____

_____

_____

_____

_____

_____

_____

_____

_____

_____

_____

_____

_____

_____

_____

_____

A mistake I'll never make again is...

My action steps for today are...

_____

_____

_____

_____

_____

_____

_____

_____

_____

_____

_____

_____

_____

_____

_____

_____

_____

Today I want to learn...

_____

_____

_____

_____

_____

_____

_____

_____

_____

_____

_____

_____

_____

_____

_____

_____

Two Duncan Nuggets®
On Making Excuses

Duncan Nugget® #111
Regardless of your age, race, gender, or circumstances there are two words that will carry you to success:

Duncan Nugget® #110
You can make an excuse or you can make a way, but you can't do both.

HEY! Remember to check out the video for this page.
http://duncannuggets.com/success-journal-videos

An excuse that I will stop making is...

_____

_____

_____

_____

_____

_____

_____

_____

_____

_____

_____

_____

_____

_____

_____

Today I plan to...

_____

_____

_____

_____

_____

_____

_____

_____

_____

_____

_____

_____

_____

_____

_____

_____

_____

3 Things I will do to be a better leader are...

_____

_____

_____

_____

_____

_____

_____

_____

_____

_____

_____

_____

_____

_____

_____

_____

My goal for today is...

_____

_____

_____

_____

_____

_____

_____

_____

_____

_____

_____

_____

_____

_____

_____

_____

Duncan Nugget® #40:
For the Haters and the Doubters

When the haters and doubters show up in your life (they always do) and when you experience pain and adversity, sometimes the only things you have to keep you going are your prayers, your dreams, and your goals.

Being able to pick up your success journal and read through the things you are determined to accomplish can be just the motivation and inspiration you need to keep going.

Regardless of what anyone—especially haters and doubters—thinks about you, realize that...

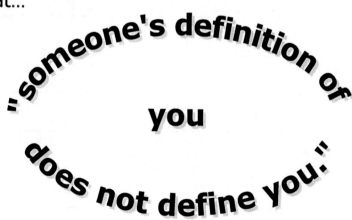

"someone's definition of you does not define you."

HEY! Remember to check out the video for this page.
http://duncannuggets.com/success-journal-videos

The thing I do to deal with haters is...

_____

_____

_____

_____

_____

_____

_____

_____

_____

_____

_____

_____

_____

_____

_____

_____

Today I want to getter better at...

_____

_____

_____

_____

_____

_____

_____

_____

_____

_____

_____

_____

_____

_____

_____

Today I am going to focus on...

_____

_____

_____

_____

_____

_____

_____

_____

_____

_____

_____

_____

_____

_____

_____

_____

3 things I will do to make better decisions are...

_____

_____

_____

_____

_____

_____

_____

_____

_____

_____

_____

_____

_____

_____

The Fog of Worry

Earl Nightingale, known to many as "The Dean of Personal Development", wrote about what he called the "Fog of Worry" and provided an authoritative estimate of what most people worry about.

- ✓ 40% of the things you worry about will never happen.
- ✓ 30% of the things you worry about couldn't be changed by all the worrying in the world.
- ✓ 12% of your worries are needless worries about your health.
- ✓ 10% of your worries are about petty, miscellaneous things.
- ✓ 8% of your worries are about real and legitimate concerns.

In other words, 92% of your worrying is a complete waste of time. Think about that.

One thing I'm going to stop worrying about is...

_____

_____

_____

_____

_____

_____

_____

_____

_____

_____

_____

_____

_____

_____

_____

My action steps for today are...

I will stop wasting my time on...

_____

_____

_____

_____

_____

_____

_____

_____

_____

_____

_____

_____

_____

_____

_____

I will do a better job of...

_____

_____

_____

_____

_____

_____

_____

_____

_____

_____

_____

_____

_____

_____

_____

_____

7 Questions
to Keep You on Point

Q: *Mr. Duncan, how do you stay on point? How do you make sure that if you're on the road to success nobody can pull you off?*

A: One of the harshest realties is: *How your life turns out is all on you. No excuses.*

People and the environment have a significant impact on your development, but for the most part you have control over where you go and the people that play a major role in your life— especially your friends and peers. **You have complete control over your attitude about what happens to you.**

Here are a set of questions that I ask myself at least once a month to make sure that I have the right attitude and stay in a state of constant elevation. Answering them in writing will help bring clarity and keep you focused.

1. With whom am I spending most of my time?
2. How are they influencing my behavior?
3. How are they influencing my thinking?
4. How are they influencing what I say?
5. How are they influencing my health? (Are they stressing me out? Are they abusive in any way?)
6. What are they influencing me to believe?

Million-Dollar Question:
Are all of these things helping me to get better and stay on point?

If the answer to the million-dollar question is "no" then it's time to change the people with whom you spend most of your time. I know that's not easy, but who ever said success was easy?

HEY! Remember to check out the video for this page.
http://duncannuggets.com/success-journal-videos

One thing I like about my success journal is...

_____

_____

_____

_____

_____

_____

_____

_____

_____

_____

_____

_____

_____

_____

_____

The thing I'm going to stop focusing on is...

---

3 things I will work on to make me a better team player are...

_____

_____

_____

_____

_____

_____

_____

_____

_____

_____

_____

_____

_____

_____

3 things I'll do to be a better student are...

_____

_____

_____

_____

_____

_____

_____

_____

_____

_____

_____

_____

_____

_____

_____

Duncan Nugget® #106
Become Exceptional

It might be time to cut back on some things in your life that you only do at an average level, so that you can spend more time becoming exceptional at one or two things.

Easier said then done?

Hey...it's called exceptional for a reason.

Exceptional people make more money.

Exceptional people have more time freedom.

Exceptional people tend to be healthier and lead more fulfilled lives.

Million-Dollar Question:
What do you do at an
exceptional level?

If you answered "nothing" or "I don't know", then cut back on something (like TV) and work on becoming exceptional at something.

HEY! Remember to check out the video for this page.
http://duncannuggets.com/success-journal-videos

My action steps for today are...

_____

_____

_____

_____

_____

_____

_____

_____

_____

_____

_____

_____

_____

_____

_____

I refuse to allow anything to stop me from...

_____

_____

_____

_____

_____

_____

_____

_____

_____

_____

_____

_____

_____

_____

_____

_____

Today is going to be awesome because...

_____

_____

_____

_____

_____

_____

_____

_____

_____

_____

_____

_____

_____

_____

_____

_____

One thing I can do to help someone else is...

_____

_____

_____

_____

_____

_____

_____

_____

_____

_____

_____

_____

_____

_____

_____

_____

Duncan Nugget® #31:
Get Your Work Done Faster

Before you go to sleep every night plan (in writing) the ACTIONS you will take tomorrow.

This increases your focus and productivity because it keeps you from *thinking* about what you're supposed to be doing and actually *doing* what you're supposed to be doing.

Do this and you will find that you get your work done faster...that means you'll have more time to do what you really want to do.

"Plan tomorrow's actions today."

HEY! Remember to check out the video for this page.
http://duncannuggets.com/success-journal-videos

3 things I am going to get done tomorrow are...

_____

_____

_____

_____

_____

_____

_____

_____

_____

_____

_____

_____

_____

_____

_____

_____

Today is going to be awesome because...

_____

_____

_____

_____

_____

_____

_____

_____

_____

_____

_____

_____

_____

_____

Today I am going to make someone smile by....

_____

_____

_____

_____

_____

_____

_____

_____

_____

_____

_____

_____

_____

_____

_____

_____

I am determined to...

Visualize Your Victory

**I
would close
my eyes and I
would start envisioning.
And this is a very powerful tool.
I can definitely say that I would never be
standing in front of you all today if I never
envisioned.**

Those are the words of Dominique Dawes, the first African-American gymnast to win an individual Olympic medal and a member of the 1996 gold medal winning Olympic U.S. Women's Gymnastics team. Dawes and a plethora of successful people from all walks of life will tell you that they had to see it before they could be it.

Your unconscious mind makes no distinction between imagination and reality. Think about that. If you imagine having confidence then you will actually experience being confident.

Whether it's a career fair or a networking event, an interview or internship, a review board or a meeting with venture capitalists, or even a date, take some time to visualize your victory.

Find a quiet place and for a few moments imagine what you will see, hear, feel, taste, and smell during your victory. Envision yourself successfully achieving your desired outcome. The more detailed your visualization, the more powerful it will be. By doing this daily you will also have more confidence in unexpected situations.

It's easier to visualize your victory when you commit to proper prior preparation. (Try saying that three times in row as fast as you can!)

HEY! Remember to check out the video for this page.
http://duncannuggets.com/success-journal-videos

My vision for my future is...

_____

_____

_____

_____

_____

_____

_____

_____

_____

_____

_____

_____

_____

_____

_____

_____

Today I plan to improve my skills by...

_____

_____

_____

_____

_____

_____

_____

_____

_____

_____

_____

_____

_____

_____

_____

_____

_____

Today I plan to accomplish these 3 things...

One idea I am going to start working on is...

_____

_____

_____

_____

_____

_____

_____

_____

_____

_____

_____

_____

_____

Duncan Nugget® #67
Young and Successful

Greatness has no age. Regardless of how old you are you can do great things. It's never too early. Some of the greatest ideas and inventions in the history of the world have come from young people like you.

Got an idea for a business?

Start it. Now.

Got an idea for an invention?

Work on it. Now.

Got an idea for a community service project?

Do it. Now.

Million-Dollar Question:
Are you ready to be successful...now?

HEY! Remember to check out the video for this chapter.
http://duncannuggets.com/success-journal-videos

I believe I am going to be successful because...

Today I want to getter better at...

_____

_____

_____

_____

_____

_____

_____

_____

_____

_____

_____

_____

_____

_____

_____

_____

I refuse to allow failure to stop me because...

_____

_____

_____

_____

_____

_____

_____

_____

_____

_____

_____

_____

_____

_____

_____

What I do to get myself motivated is...

_____

_____

_____

_____

_____

_____

_____

_____

_____

_____

_____

_____

_____

_____

_____

_____

_____

Challenge Your
Beliefs and Perceptions

Your beliefs and perceptions
determine the boundaries of your world.

Think about that. When you challenge or change your beliefs and perceptions, you're altering your concept of reality. You are changing your world. If you understand what I'm saying, then you'll understand why it's so hard for people to give up certain beliefs and perceptions.

People rarely seek information that contradicts what they believe. In fact, it's not unusual for people to completely ignore evidence that refutes what they believe. They tend to look for anything that validates and reinforces their beliefs.

If you were hanging off of a cliff and the only thing keeping you from falling was the rope you were holding on to, how tightly would you hold on to that rope?

You probably hold on to most of your beliefs the same way.

Once you believe that your anger is justified (and it might be), it can be incredibly challenging to let go of that belief. Once you have a perception that someone has intentionally said or done something negative to you (and he may have) it can be extremely difficult to let go of that belief, but the bottom line is:

Duncan Nugget® #192
Mastering your anger requires that you challenge your beliefs and perceptions.

HEY! Remember to check out the video for this page.
http://duncannuggets.com/success-journal-videos

One thing that makes me unique is...

_____

_____

_____

_____

_____

_____

_____

_____

_____

_____

_____

_____

_____

_____

_____

_____

When I'm feeling lazy, the thing that I use to get myself motivated is...

_____

_____

_____

_____

_____

_____

_____

_____

_____

_____

_____

_____

_____

_____

The thing I like best about me is...

_____

_____

_____

_____

_____

_____

_____

_____

_____

_____

_____

_____

_____

_____

_____

My goal for today is...

_____

_____

_____

_____

_____

_____

_____

_____

_____

_____

_____

_____

_____

_____

_____

_____

Thoroughly Prepare and Be Authentic

One of my mentors told me a story about a guy who talked his way into a high level position for which he was unprepared. On the first day of work the guy was sitting in his corner office feeling unconfident and trying to figure out how he was going to pull off this caper when he heard a knock at his door.

"Just a minute," he hollered. While jumping behind his desk he told the person knocking to come in. He picked up the phone started and pretending that he was having a conversation with the CEO of the company.

"Yes sir, Mr. Johnson. I'll take care of it", he told the imaginary CEO on the phone while using his index finger to give a 'wait a minute' sign to the gentleman who had just walked into his office.

"I know the company's future is riding on this, Mr. Johnson. You can count on me. Good bye."

He hung up the phone and turned his attention to the gentleman in his office. "How can I help you?"

With a big grin on his face, the gentleman responded, "I'm here to connect your phone service."

Long before anyone else does, you know if you've properly prepared for the task at hand. It's difficult to be confident when you're not prepared and pretending to be something that you're not. Thoroughly prepare and keep it real. Be authentic.

HEY! Remember to check out the video for this article.
http://duncannuggets.com/success-journal-videos

Today I am going to focus on...

_____

_____

_____

_____

_____

_____

_____

_____

_____

_____

_____

_____

_____

_____

_____

A lesson I learned from someone I admire is...

I get my work done because...

_____

_____

_____

_____

_____

_____

_____

_____

_____

_____

_____

_____

_____

_____

_____

_____

One place I plan to travel to is...

_____

_____

_____

_____

_____

_____

_____

_____

_____

_____

_____

_____

_____

_____

_____

Duncan Nugget® #47
Focus on Your Strengths

One of the secrets of success is to constantly get better at what you do best and learn to manage or delegate when it comes to your weaknesses.

Spend some of your time focusing on your weaknesses; spend MOST of your time focusing on your strengths.

In other words, focus more on what you CAN do and focus less on what you can't do. It's not a question of "what's wrong with you?"

Million-Dollar Question:
"What's RIGHT with you?"

HEY! Remember to check out the video for this page.
http://duncannuggets.com/success-journal-videos

One thing I will do to improve my strengths is...

_____

_____

_____

_____

_____

_____

_____

_____

_____

_____

_____

_____

_____

_____

_____

Today I plan to...

My action steps for today are...

_____

_____

_____

_____

_____

_____

_____

_____

_____

_____

_____

_____

_____

_____

I will work on my communication skills by...

_____

_____

_____

_____

_____

_____

_____

_____

_____

_____

_____

_____

_____

_____

How to Get Something for Nothing

"Men may not get all they pay for in this world,
but they must certainly pay for all they get."
–*Frederick Douglass*

Well. I'm waiting. Waiting for what? I'm waiting for the answer, of course. Oh, wait a minute. Did you think I was going to show you how to get something for nothing? Actually, the title of this article is more like a question directed to YOU. And if you know the answer, I don't even want to know. But there is an ocean of other ears that would love to hear from you! So many people want the juice but they don't want to grow the tree, pick the fruit, peel the orange, juice it, and bottle it up.

That's perfectly fine and dandy when you can go to the store and buy some juice, but fortunately (no, I don't mean unfortunately) you can't just go to the store and buy a quart of success or liter of happiness. I'm sure that you already know that success and happiness come with a price tag or you wouldn't be reading this article. Just like we put money off to the side to save up to buy things we want, successful people put extra time in on the side to create the lifestyle they want. They pay the price.

Is it going to kill you to invest an extra hour or two in your dream? How about investing some extra time in your family or whatever's important to you? It's been said that you earn a living from 9 to 5 and you make a fortune from 5 to 9. Think about that.

Self-empowerment has a price. Financial empowerment has a price. Success, fulfillment, and well-being all have a price that has nothing to do with money. It has everything to do with commitment and diligence. If you know how to get something for nothing, do yourself a favor and pretend you don't know. Pay the price to get what you want out of life. It's worth it.

HEY! Remember to check out the video for this article.
http://duncannuggets.com/success-journal-videos

I will pay the price to be successful because...

_____

_____

_____

_____

_____

_____

_____

_____

_____

_____

_____

_____

_____

_____

_____

_____

I am unstoppable because...

_____

_____

_____

_____

_____

_____

_____

_____

_____

_____

_____

_____

_____

_____

_____

_____

People who know me say I'm great at...

_____

_____

_____

_____

_____

_____

_____

_____

_____

_____

_____

_____

_____

_____

3 smart things I will do with my money are...

Duncan Nugget® #17
A Broken Way of Life

One of the keys to greatness is finding a way to do something you love to do, not just something that's "safe" to do. Many people have experienced a high level of achievement but are stuck in professions they hate.

What kind of sense does that make?

None.

"High achievement without fulfillment is a broken way of life."

HEY! Remember to check out the video for this article.
http://duncannuggets.com/success-journal-videos

Working on my goals makes me happy because...

_____

_____

_____

_____

_____

_____

_____

_____

_____

_____

_____

_____

_____

_____

What I like best about myself is...

Today I plan to accomplish these 3 things...

_____

_____

_____

_____

_____

_____

_____

_____

_____

_____

_____

_____

_____

_____

_____

_____

The next time something or someone is frustrating me, what I will do to feel better is...

_____

_____

_____

_____

_____

_____

_____

_____

_____

_____

_____

_____

_____

_____

Duncan Nugget® #223
Who's in Control?

Identify what is and what is not under your control.

Billionaire insurance executive A.L. Williams once said, "All you can do is all you can do. And all you can do is enough. But you better make sure you do all you can do."

After a setback many people spend too much time agonizing over things they have little or no control over. So when you are preparing for the interview or whatever the opportunity may be, take inventory of what is and isn't directly under your control.

Make a list of everything that has to happen in order for your opportunity to become a successful endeavor. After completing your list go through it and label each item as under your control or not under your control.

For instance, being well prepared for an interview is under your control. Being the most qualified and experienced person for the job isn't under your control. There's no way for you to know who else is being interviewed for the position.

WARNING: Be careful of passing the buck or playing the blame game. You've got to be honest with yourself about your assessment of what is and isn't under your control.

Million-Dollar Question:
Who's in control? Really?

HEY! Remember to check out the video for this article.
http://duncannuggets.com/success-journal-videos

204 | Al Duncan

My action steps for today are...

_____

_____

_____

_____

_____

_____

_____

_____

_____

_____

_____

_____

_____

_____

_____

_____

Today I plan to...

Today I am going to focus on...

_____

_____

_____

_____

_____

_____

_____

_____

_____

_____

_____

_____

_____

_____

_____

_____

_____

Today I want to getter better at...

_____

_____

_____

_____

_____

_____

_____

_____

_____

_____

_____

_____

_____

_____

_____

It's About Time

Whether it's quality time, playtime, game time, family time, me-time, real time, study time, daytime, nighttime, wrong time, or the right time, one thing is for sure...

Sometimes it seems as if life is all about time, doesn't it?

Here are a few nuggets adapted from a series of articles I wrote titled *"A State Mind Called Time"*. These principles have nothing to do with a calendar, planner, iPhone, Blackberry, or any other gadget. These principles are about your state of mind. If your philosophy about time isn't right, typical time management tools won't even do you any good.

Duncan Nugget® #181
You do not find time; you make time.

People love to say, "if I could just find the time..."

NEWS FLASH: You will never find time.

Can you just walk down the street, find an extra hour that somebody lost, and add it to your day? Of course not. So, if there is something you want to accomplish or do then MAKE the time to do it.

Duncan Nugget® #182
Stop spending your time;
start investing your time.

"Time is money."

If that's true, then shouldn't there be Return On Investment (ROI) for your time? Shouldn't you get something in exchange for giving someone or something some of your time? It doesn't have to be money, but it should be something of value.

Million-Dollar Question:
What have you been getting in return for your time?

Write down five things you've done recently. What did you get in return?

Knowledge?

Peace of mind?

Money?

Happiness?

I seriously hope your answer isn't "I don't know."

Duncan Nugget® #183
Respect Time...or else.

Do I really have to explain this? If Father Time could talk he would be outraged. He's had his civil rights violated more than anybody. If he had legs, people would be getting their butts kicked on a regular basis!

When you disrespect Father Time, he will get even. Instead of being in the right place at the right time, opportunities slip right through your fingers. Or you do things like miss your bus or flight by 5 minutes. Not cool. Respect Father Time and he will reward you greatly. And...

Never let someone disrespect your time.

——————————
HEY! Remember to check out the video for this article. http://duncannuggets.com/success-journal-videos

Today I will invest my time in...

_____

_____

_____

_____

_____

_____

_____

_____

_____

_____

_____

_____

_____

_____

Duncan Nugget® #11
The Enemy Within

The ability to achieve success begins and ends with your state of mind.

If you've done all of the exercises in this book, and stuck to your GPS—**Guiding Principles for Success**—then you are well on your way to living a life of abundance.

Most of the obstacles that people face in life are self-imposed. So, be on a constant look out for the only person who can stop you—the enemy within. Continue to write down what you want out of life and what it takes to get it.

And always remember that...

"You are guaranteed to win once you defeat the enemy within because... It's ALL Mental!"

HEY! Remember to check out the video for this article. http://duncannuggets.com/success-journal-videos

Some Good Books for You to Check Out

Soft Skills/Personal Development

- *My Career Journal: The Young Person's Guide To Having An Awesome Career* by Al Duncan
- *The 7 Habits of Highly Effective Teens* by Sean Covey
- *The 6 Most Important Decisions You'll Ever Make* by Sean Covey
- *Making College Count (Second Edition)* by Patrick O'Brien
- *How to Win Friends & Influence People* by Dale Carnegie
- *Think and Grow Rich* by Napoleon Hill
- *Think and Grow Rich: A Black Choice* by Dennis Kimbro & Napoleon Hill
- *The Greatest Salesman in the World* by Og Mandino
- *Get ALL Fired Up! About Living Your Dreams (Revised Edition)* by Al Duncan

Entrepreneurship/Money

- *The Richest Man in Babylon* by George S. Clason
- *Campus CEO: The Student Entrepreneur's Guide to Launching a Multi-Million-Dollar Business* by Randal Pinkett

Al Duncan is an award-winning youth advocate, publisher, and internationally recognized authority on soft skills, youth development and empowerment.

He is the publisher of **DuncanNuggets.com** a resource center packed with free videos, articles, and activities on character education and soft skills. As the leading motivational speaker for at-risk youth and troubled young people, Al has delivered his **Duncan Nuggets®** live and in-person to *over 1 million young people around the world.*

He is the author of *My Success Journal For Young People* and *Get ALL Fired Up!* He has been awarded the National PTA Life Achievement Award and the President's Call to Service Award, for his outstanding service in the field of youth development and empowerment.

Formerly, as a corporate trainer he has delivered his programs as professional development courses at a number of colleges and universities including the University of Georgia Center for Continuing Education and Professional Development.

Devastated, But Not Defeated

Al was born and raised in a dangerous, poverty stricken neighborhood in North Philadelphia and by today's standards, would've been labeled an "at-risk" student. When he was 5 years old he was molested by a male friend of the family. Emotionally traumatized, it took him years to remember what happened. At the age of 15, Al's world was torn to shreds again when he found out that his father, his childhood hero, was addicted to crack cocaine. Devastated, but not defeated, Al refused to allow his personal problems stop him. He went on to enjoy careers as a professional saxophone player and a professional chef. His father's struggle and incredible recovery inspired Al to write Duncan Nugget® #21: Failure is only permanent if you quit.

At the age of 24, he walked away from his musical career and took on the tremendous responsibility of raising his youngest brother who was 12 years old at the time.

Today, Al's expertise in the fields of soft skills, leadership, youth development & empowerment has been sought after by a long list of organizations and institutions.

CPSIA information can be obtained
at www.ICGtesting.com
Printed in the USA
FFOW05n0800210915